Come Fly With Me!

Your Nineties Guide to Becoming a Flight Attendant

By Reginald Dunlop

Maxamillian Publishing, Chicago

Come Fly With Me !

Your Nineties Guide to Becoming a Flight Attendant

By Reginald Dunlop

Published by:

Maxamillian Publishing
Post Office Box 10034
Chicago, IL 60610 U.S.A.

Library of Congress Cataloging in Publication Data

Dunlop, Reginald M.
Come Fly With Me ! : Your Nineties Guide to Becoming a Flight Attendant / Reginald Dunlop -1st ed.

Edited by : Alisa Bennett-Hart, Charles Berstein
Illustrations: Cornelious Ward

Includes Index.
1. Careers
2. Aviation
3. Airlines

Library of Congress Catalog Card Number: 92-060674

ISBN 0-9632749-9-6

Printed in the United States of America

Acknowledgements

I must first give thanks to God who has guided me throughout the completion of this project and to whom I have prayed will bless all who use this guide with success and prosperity.

It is imperative to have a supportive group of friends and family to make any book possible. It is those people in particular who have been optimistic supporters from the onset whom I appreciate the most.

I would like to give special thanks to :

Geneva Spigner : Your support and enthusiasm were key factors in my transition from talk to reality.

Alisa Bennet-Hart : Thank you for your editing work and your help in getting me out of the stone age.

Fran Kosac Design : You have been absolutely wonderful. I can not say enough about how much I love your artwork and your style of doing business.

Dee McConnell : Thanks for your help on "Health and Beauty" and all of the positive motivation.

Cornelious Ward : Thanks for all of your help, it was fun working together. I bought you a new belt.

Fred Diggs : I believed that you are the first person who I pulled into this project. Thanks. I bet that I can still get around Yales' library !

Molly Norwood : I would like to thank you and all of the people at Blue Ribbon Press for your encouragement and technical expertise. You put the icing on the cake.

Thanks to everyone who made special contributions: Bruce Spigner, Jackie Hinton, Nelson Hart and all of my friends at United Airlines and The BAP Group International. I am eternally grateful.

One dollar from the sale of this book will be donated to religious charities and organizations devoted to enhancing the opportunities for our youth. A list of these charities will be provided upon request.

Maxamillian Publishing

CONTENTS

Chapter 1
The Airline Industry

Chapter 1- The Airline Industry

When you join the airline industry, you have chosen to be a part of a fine American tradition. The industry has become one of the fastest growing in the world. Let us take a brief look at aviation history in the United States.

During the late eighteen-hundreds, numerous young inventors excited the world as they took to the skies in their fabulous flying machines. Their goal was to make air travel a viable means of transportation. While they produced bigger and more reliable aircraft, entrepreneurs began to view the airplane as an exciting new making money machine. They pondered numerous uses for the airplane from towing banners and herding sheep to carrying mail and passengers.

The first profitable businesses to emerge were air-mail carriers. By 1918 this country had its first regularly scheduled airmail service. Airmail immediately replaced slower methods of mail delivery like the train and the Pony Express.

As small air carriers merged and expanded to handle larger postal contracts, these growing airlines became quite diverse. Many of these companies carried mail, operated flight schools, crop dusting operations, and some began to carry passengers. By 1925 this country had its first regularly scheduled passenger airline service. Demand for passenger service exploded, and airlines responded by expanding to meet rising passenger demands.

Even though it was quite evident that air travel would become the dominant mode of transportation, the majority of the population was still uncomfortable with the idea of riding on airplanes. The chief concern was the reliability and safety of aircraft. Much of this uneasiness disappeared in 1927 when Charles Lindbergh thrilled the world by flying his aircraft, "The Spirit-Of-St. Louis", from New York to Paris thus becoming the first man to cross the Atlantic in an airplane. When he arrived in Paris, he was greeted with a hero's welcome. This spectacular event sent aviation interest soaring! The demand for passenger flights practically doubled overnight. Immediately it became very fashionable to travel by air. The newspapers often photographed celebrities boarding airplanes to exotic destinations. Airlines responded to this new demand by ordering new airplanes and altering service as passengers replaced mail as their primary payload.

Around 1930 Boeing Air Transport

to become United Airlines) revolutionized customer service in the airline industry when they hired nurse Ellen Church Marshall to become the first airline stewardess. Passenger acceptance of the stewardess was overwhelming. Passengers found it reassuring to have a registered nurse in the cabin to tend to their needs.

Rapid growth in the industry continued throughout the thirties. Many smaller carriers merged to compete for lucrative government contracts which called for a transcontinental airline. In 1938, the Civil Aeronautics Authority (CAA) was created to regulate the aviation industry. While the CAA performed many duties, they primarily functioned as a governing body to decide which routes an airline could fly and what fares that they could charge.

In 1960, the jet age for commercial aviation was born. Jet aircraft quickly became part of most airline fleets replacing propeller-driven aircraft. Passenger acceptance of jets was immediate. Airlines promoted the jets increased speed, dependability, and additional passenger comfort.

Throughout the late seventies and eighties, times were very turbulent for the already volatile airline industry. Not only was the economy in a slump, rising fuel costs began to hurt most carriers. Many airlines sold their inefficient aircraft and laid off their employees to cut losses.

During the mid-seventies, public resentment towards government intervention and the bureaucratic process was peaking. It was popular for politicians to advocate less government and the dismantling of regulatory agencies. This mode of thinking suggested that a deregulated airline industry would serve the public better by opening the doors to more competition. Competition which would both increase service and lower airfares. In the late 1970s, Senator Edward Kennedy chaired a committee to discuss the deregulation of the airline industry. The findings of that meeting and the changing political climate, led to the signing of the deregulation act of 1978. This action sent the airline industry into a state of turmoil. No longer could the major airlines enjoy a monopoly on routes and controlled airfares.

Without the barriers of controlled routes and fares, the skies were open for competition. New airlines such as People Express, Midway, America West and Southwest became successful by offering extremely low airfares. As competition became heated, fares dropped to such a level that everyone in the industry lost money, especially the larger carriers that required much higher fares just to break even.

As the eighties progressed, the big carriers responded to their new environment very aggressively by cutting costs on all levels. They eliminated jobs, decreased passenger amenities, reduced food service, added more seats to their airplanes, and yes, they even cut employee salaries and benefits. This brutal cost-cutting measure produced the most divisive and demoralizing element to face organized labor, the B-Scale. The B-scale, or two-tier pay system is a pay structure that requires new employees to work for dramatically lower wages than their senior counterparts. The hostility surrounding the B-scale is responsible for decreased employee moral and several work stoppages or strikes.

The larger airlines, through decreased operating costs and elaborate yield-management computers, were able to reduce cost to a minimum. Even with reduced cost, the major carriers were still losing money because nearly bankrupt competitors were charging outrageously low fares just to generate cash flow. The only way to stop this heated competition was for a carrier to buy its' competitor. This spurred an airline merger mania. Larger airlines began to consume their competitors resulting in less competition and higher airfares.

By the late eighties, stability returned to the industry with only a handful of airlines emerging from deregulation. Many airlines soon shifted back into profit-making and refocused efforts on areas such as customer service and employee relations. By the end of the decade, most companies reaped record profits and ordered new equipment at an unprecedented rate.

Airlines aggressively expanded overseas to serve the needs of a new global economy. This dynamic expansion continues to take airline hiring to record heights, resulting in quick and rapid promotions.

It is clear that this past decade and the nineties will indeed prove to be the best time in history to start an airline career! It is exciting to see how quickly this industry and its technology have evolved in a relatively short period of time. A mere 30 years ago, major airline fleets were comprised solely of propeller-driven aircraft. Just imagine how this industry will operate in the next 30 years!

Airplanes currently under development are being designed to answer the needs of a changing society. Airplanes are now being tested which can hover like a helicopter to fly into the heart of major metropolitan areas or to fly at speeds of over 3,000 miles per hour so a person could travel from New York to Tokyo in just four hours. In 1995, Boeing will introduce an airplane which will be equipped with collapsible wings to help conserve space on the ground at many of today's already congested airports! Come join the thousands who are already a part of this progressive and rewarding industry. Welcome aboard !

Chapter 2
The Airline Lifestyle

Your main responsibilities as a flight attendant are to insure the safety and comfort of your passengers. As an ambassador of your company, whenever you wear your uniform you are expected to exercise professionalism and a positive public image. The airlines are only seeking individuals who they feel can display competency, confidence, and a sincere desire to provide superior service for their valued customers.

A flight attendant's responsibilities are quite extensive and include the following duties: performing safety demonstrations and announcements, checking emergency equipment, greeting and directing customers, serving meals and drinks, providing passengers with blankets and pillows, answering questions, assisting handicapped passengers and minors, and working efficiently with the rest of the crew.

Oh that glamorous lifestyle! Professional flight attendants are envied by many who view them as mysterious and well-dressed people who glide through the airport terminals with an intimate knowledge of the world. It is a job which garners pride and respect. Everyone will want to know where you have just flown in from and where you are going next.

Working for an airline is comparable to joining an elite club. You will form unique friendships with other flight attendants and the interesting people whom you will meet around the world. You will have the opportunity to meet professional athletes, celebrities and politicians. Its a lifestyle and a daily experience that is so unique that you will never want to return to a regular (boring) routine.

What's it like? It is different every day. On some days, you must report for duty at the crack of dawn, while other times you might not start work until the early afternoon or evening. There are days that you might work as little as 2 hours or other days when you must work 12 hours. Its the variety of the position that many people find so appealing.

Each month, the company publishes hundreds of lines (monthly schedules) for you to bid on. These lines allow an average of fifteen days off per month. The monthly time off for flight attendants ranges from 12-20 days off. As time passes and you gain seniority, you can choose trips that are tailor-made to fit your lifestyle. With this type of versatility, you will find that many flight attendants engage in a variety of outside activities. Many flight attendants work either 2-3 day trips on weekends in order to have weekdays free to pursue their own personal interests such as attending college, selling real estate or performing charity work. Attending school works out extremely well, because there is so much time to study on layovers. Married people generally prefer trips during the week to maximize the time that they have at home on weekends to spend with their families. You can also bid for trips that have long layovers where your friends and relatives live. Why not find a trip with a long layover in a city that you have never seen and do some sightseeing while you are getting paid?

Let us examine an average monthly line of flying and pretend that line 194 on the following page represents your line for the month.

MONTHLY LINE OF FLYING

line 194 Cr. 69.24 Blk. 69.24 Days Off 18 3 F/A

02	03	04	05	06	07	08	09	10	11	12	13	14	15	16	17	18	19	20	21	22	23	24	25	26	27	28	29	30	31
FR	SA	SU	MO	TU	WE	TH	FR	SA	SU	MO	TU	WE	TH	FR	SA	SU	MO	TU	WE	TH	FR	SA	SU	MO	TU	WE	TH	FR	SA
				758						758							758							758					
				TYS PBI ORD						TYS PBI ORD							TYS PBI ORD							TYS ORD					

758=0700 / 1807

As you can see, this schedule begins on the 2nd. This is done for scheduling purposes so that all lines have 30 days. You are off the first 4 days of the month. Your first workday begins on Tuesday the sixth with trip ID number 758. A trip ID is a number assigned to a particular trip sequence. Lets examine a three day trip ID 758 on the following page.

3-DAY TRIP SEQUENCE

ID 0758 (TRIP I.D. NUMBER) EFF 03/01/92 THRU 03/31/92 ID# 075837B

TRIP I.D. NUMBER	FLIGHT NUMBER	DEPARTURE CITY	DESTINATION	DEPARTURE TIME	ARRIVAL TIME	LAYOVER TIME	FLIGHT TIME	CUMULATIVE FLIGHT TIME FOR THE DAY
37B	328	ORD	RDU	0700	0948	.51	1.48	1.48
37B	873	RDU	ORD	1039	1143	2.50	2.04	3.52
37B	280	ORD	TYS	1433	1701	14.04	1.28	5.20
					HYATT REGENCY (LAYOVER HOTEL)		615-123-1234	
37B	755	TYS	ORD	0705	0737	.53	1.32	1.32
37B	596	ORD	PBI	0830	1225	19.49	2.55	4.27
					PALM BEACH LAKES		407-123-1234	
37B	597	PBI	ORD	0814	1020	1.05	3.06	3.06
27E	296	ORD	BDL	1125	1423	2.14	1.58	5.04
27E	955	BDL	ORD	1637	1807		2.30	7.34

BID-17.21* TTL-17.21* (PROJECTED FLIGHT TIME) TMA- 60.37 (TIME AWAY FROM BASE) M/$ 90.93 (EXPENSE ALLOWANCE)

Your first flight #328 from Chicago, IL to Raleigh, NC departs O'Hare airport at 0700 hours. (See the glossary for military clock.) For a 0700 departure, you must arrive at the airport at 0600 to check in. At 0600, you will meet with your crew in the lounge for a briefing. During the briefing, you will discuss issues concerning the trip such as who will fly which positions, the type of service on the flights, any new company policies or procedures. The briefing usually lasts about 15 minutes. From there, you will proceed to the airplane. At the airplane you will meet the cockpit crew. The captain will give a quick briefing about flight conditions, weather and any other special considerations for the day.

Now its time to inspect the cabin. Your safety inspection involves checking to see that all safety equipment is present and in good working condition. You must check to see that the cabin service crew has properly serviced the aircraft. You must also check your galleys to assure that food service has supplied you with appropriate meals and refreshments.

Now it is time for boarding. One flight attendant will go to the boarding area to take passenger tickets while the other attendants take their positions on board the aircraft to greet and assist passengers. A few minutes prior to departure time, the gate agent will board the airplane to make a final departure announcement and close the door.

While taxiing to the runway, the flight attendants will perform a short safety demonstration prior to taking their stations for departure. Shortly after takeoff, you wheel out the carts to serve breakfast and drinks. After everyone has eaten, meal trays are picked up and coffee or additional refreshments are served. Typically while enroute, you circulate throughout the cabin to assist the passengers . Prior to descent you will make a report on any money received from liquor or movie sales. In preparation for landing, the flight attendants will check to assure that the passenger seats are in their proper positions and the galleys are secure. Sometimes while the passengers are deplaning you may be asked to assist an elderly or handicapped person.

As you can see, from ID 758, you'll be on the ground in Raleigh for 51 minutes before working your trip back to Chicago. Once in Chicago, you have 2 hours and fifty minutes of layover time for a break. Now its on to Knoxville, TN for a14 hour and four minute layover.

On layovers, the company provides a hotel, transportation and a per diem to cover your meal expenses.

The next day is fairly easy. You will take flight 755 to Chicago, then flight 596 to Palm Beach, FL for a 19.47-hour layover. The trip ends the next night at 1807 hours.

You are now off for the next four days to relax at home, travel or do whatever you wish. Well, that was a typical 3- day trip. There are tougher trips that have five-leg days and other trips that might have one leg to Honolulu with a 2-day layover. By now you should understand that being a flight attendant can be physically demanding, stressful, yet enjoyable and adventurous. All things considered, job satisfaction among flight attendants is very high. Once you become hooked on the lifestyle, it is very difficult to return to a normal routine.

Chapter 3
Choosing An Employer

There are many methods that people use in selecting an employer. The most logical way is to assess your reasons for becoming a flight attendant and to select a company capable of fulfilling your needs. We have outlined six major considerations for choosing an employer.

Financial Strength

If you are planning a career as a flight attendant the financial strength of the organization is very important. If your goal is long-term employment security you must find an employer who is financially sound. Such a company would be termed solvent, which means that the company is capable of paying all of it's financial responsibilities and still have money for growth. A company's solvency directly affects it's ability to pay good wages, maintain employee benefits and remain a progressive business entity.

Most libraries carry Moody's Transportation Index, an excellent reference periodical that lists a particular company's financial stability. Pay particular attention to the company's bond rating; this will tell you how lending institutions view their economic strength. Stock market figures also give a clear picture of a company's strengths and weaknesses. A stock broker can advise you of recent trends in the airline business; which company's are hot and which are involved in hostile takeovers or unfavorable litigations.

Career Advancement

It is wise to look for a company where rapid career advancement is possible. However, you must consider the reasons for this upward mobility. If the company is expanding or their senior staff is retiring, these are wholesome advancement opportunities. But if the company is not expanding or retiring senior employees, offers for employment are to be viewed with suspicion. Aggressive hiring could stem from high turnover or stacking employees in cases of a pending strike. Avoid these situations at all costs!

For obvious reasons, if you are hired as a replacement worker or scab during a strike, you may forfeit any job security. Even if the company promises you a permanent position, workers returning from the strike will be angry and they are likely to treat you with extreme hostility.

Domiciles

Location for many people is an important criteria in selecting an employer. It requires a little more work that merely reviewing the Airline section to determine if a company has a domicile where you would like to live. Even though a company has a domicile in a location where you'd like to live, you must consider the likelihood of your getting assigned to such a location.

Since getting based in a location is awarded according to seniority, it is important to know where new-hires are placed and how soon they can choose another base. In many cases, when companies have bases in very desirable locations, they are often small and require company seniority of 10 years or more. However these conditions are constantly changing. The best way to find the answers to these questions is to inquire during your interview or to ask a company employee.

Even though living at a company domicile is desirable, it is not essential. About half of all inflight personnel commute to work. This literally allows you to live anywhere that you would like to as long as it has air service. Even though commuting is widely practiced, every commuter will tell you that it is a very complicated and often stressful process which should be avoided if possible.

Route Structure

If you intend to travel extensively, finding an airline with the most extensive route structure may be your primary interest. All of the major airlines have reciprocal pass agreements with other carriers, to allow their employees to travel on these airlines at a reduced rate. However the ideal situation is to see the world while working and getting paid.

Here are some essential steps to take. First, you must identify the region of the world that you would like to visit most. Then look for the airlines which provide the best service to those areas. Next, you must find out how soon you will be eligible to fly internationally. This information can be obtained during your interview or from an employee of the airline. It would be disappointing to select a firm primarily on its international destinations, only to discover that it requires eight years seniority to fly to those destinations which you most desire.

Pay and Benefits

Most unioned airlines negotiate contracts of three to five years duration. Since pay scales usually change when new contracts are settled it is important to know when the present contract expires. Non-union contracts are subject to change at any time. During the early eighties pay and benefits were radically different as carriers adjusted to the newly competitive and deregulated environment. In the nineties pay and benefits will become more consistent throughout the industry. Presently, the most noteworthy differences between the airlines is in the area of medical and dental benefits, pass policies, holiday pay and the length of time one must remain on the B-scale. Currently first year pay at the major airlines is approximately $14,000 per year increasing to $30,000 after 5 years. Maximum flight attendant pay is over $50,000 per year.

Making a Final Choice

It is unlikely that all the airlines to which you apply will offer you employment at the same time. Since there are no guarantees that your first choice will ever offer you employment, it would be prudent to accept a position with the first stable carrier that offers you immediate employment.

Chapter 4

Do I Have What it Takes?

Who are the the people that airlines call for an interview? They call the applicants who meet both their basic and most desired qualifications. Many suitable applicants are

never called for an interview because their applications don't exhibit that they possess the qualities that the airlines consider most valuable. It is easier to sell yourself in person, but it is a real science to sell yourself within the small confines of an employment application. The secret of selling yourself on an application is to know what the employer is looking for and to make it clear that he or she has found that in you.

The following list of "Basic Qualifications" are the minimum qualifications that most airlines require. Applicants with less than these qualifications will not even be considered. The second list, called "Desired Flight Attendant Qualities", are qualities that the airlines are *really* looking for. These are the additional, often unwritten, qualities that can make the difference for an applicant getting hired.

Basic Qualifications

1. At least 19 years of age
2. High school graduate
3. Height in proportion to weight
4. Vision correctable to at least 20/40
5. Eligible to work in the United States
6. At least 5"2'
7. Fluent in English
8. Good communication skills
9. Previous employment with public contact preferred

Desired Qualifications

1. Service-oriented
2. Foreign language skills
3. Outgoing and friendly
4. Works well as a team leader/member
5. Willing to take charge
6. Exercise mature judgement
7. Good communication skills
8. Poised
9. Well-groomed
10. Handles job stress
11. Flexible
12. A sense of humor
13. Likes working with all types of people
14. Eager to assist and help others
15. Works efficiently
16. Confident
17. Caring
18. Self-motivated
19. Healthy
20. Punctual

As you can imagine, there are millions of people who meet the basic qualifications. Every week the major airlines receive over 20,000 applications. How do they choose from such a large pool? They select the applicants with the most "Desired Qualities". Perhaps they are bilingual or possess certification in nursing. Maybe they are already well-traveled or have volunteered with the Peace Corps. Whatever hidden assets which you possess must be uncovered. Highlighting your qualifications will maximize your chances of successful employment with an airline. The next section on "Highlighting your Qualifications" and "The Personal Asset Workshop" will help teach you how to spotlight your unique abilities and talents. You will probably discover that experiences which you may have never considered to be important are highly valued assets in the airline industry.

Chapter 5

Highlighting Your Qualifications

The Personal Asset Workshop (PAW)

Before corresponding with any employer, you must understand the importance of each letter, resume, and application. They are sales tools. Like brochures, flyers, and commercials, your correspondence (promotional material), must effectively sell your value and demonstrate that you can meet the needs of your customer. To do this, you must first know the needs of your customer and make all of your communications appeal to those needs. In the previous chapter "Qualifications", you learned the type of person whom airlines are looking for. In this section, you will learn how to present yourself so that you meet those needs. Your goal is to make all of your communications demonstrate that you possess most of the “Desired Flight Attendant Qualities".

The "Personal Asset Workshop" was designed to help you uncover skills, abilities, and qualifications that you possess which illustrate that you are an ideal candidate for the job. Fill in each section as completely as possible. Include activities that may seem trivial. After careful consideration, some of these seemingly insignificant activities can display very positive and desirable personality traits. Your Personal Asset Workshop will never be complete. You will find that every time you review it, you will find new things to add. At the end of your workshop you will complete a "Personal Asset Sheet". This will be a valuable reference which will help you convey the right message in all of your communications. Consult your "Personal Asset Sheet" prior to completing your application, writing a resume, or going to an interview.

Step 1 Personal Asset Workshop

Complete the Initial Worksheet. Include everything possible, this is a time to really brainstorm. Below each category, there are some examples to help give you ideas.

Personal Asset Workshop

INITIAL WORKSHEET

Previous Employment ______________________________

____

____

____

Examples: Sales clerk, child-care provider, host at a 5 star restaurant, landscaper, telemarketer, school teacher, chef or registered dietician, freelance typist, data entry technician, computer programmer, licensed practical nurse, social worker or counselor.

Certification/Licenses/Special Training ______________________________

____

____

Examples: Lifeguard, certified real estate appraiser, CPR(Cardio-pulmonary Resuscitation) certification, sign language interpreter, public speaking course at community college, Babylon School of Modeling certificate, small business administration, business start-up seminar, cosmetology license.

Clubs/Memberships/Organizations ______________________________

____

____

Examples: Scouting, Big Brothers & Sisters, Youth Ministry, Fraternity / Sorority, Snowbird Ski Club, Rotary.

Charity/Volunteer Work ______________________________

____

____

Examples: Active with United Way, weekend work at food bank, organized a local Teens Against Drunk Driving chapter, March of Dimes walkathon participant.

Hobbies/Sports ______________________________

____

____

Examples: Viewing art, painting, playing an instrument, reading,photography,camping, cooking, soft-ball, basketball,volleyball, swimming, golf, tennis or skiing.

Personal Asset Workshop

INITIAL WORKSHEET

Personal Skills/Qualities ______________________________

____

____

Example: In this section, you will list short phrases that describe your personal skills. Example: I am a good listener, I organize good parties, I am a good salesperson, I am energetic, trustworthy, responsible, well-organized, I am sympathetic.

Notes: ______________________________

Personal Asset Workshop

Desired Qualifications

1. Service-oriented
2. Foreign language skills*
3. Outgoing and friendly
4. Works well as a team leader/member
5. Willing to take charge
6. Exercise mature judgement
7. Good communication skills
8. Poised
9. Well-groomed
10. Handles job stress
11. Flexible
12. A sense of humor
13. Likes working with all types of people
14. Eager to assist and help others
15. Works efficiently
16. Confident
17. Caring
18. Self-motivated
19. Healthy
20. Punctual

Step 2

Review the basic and desired flight attendant qualities. Now review your Personal Asset Worksheet. ***Place an asterisk next to each item that demonstrates that you possess "The Desired Flight Attendant Qualities".** You can test each item on your PAW by putting it in a verifying sentence. **Example:** My sailing experience taught me how to work efficiently as a team member. Do you see how this supports quality # 4? **Example:** "My first job providing child-care was very enjoyable and educational. I love nurturing children and supporting their parents values. I learned valuable lessons in customer service in this job. I exhibited punctuality, diplomacy and reliability which made my clients trust and depend on me." This was a grand-slam. One seemingly small job like watching children can indicate that you possess at least six "Desirable Flight Attendant Qualities". Find them. 1, 5, 6,14, 17 and 20. **Complete your verifying sentences on the following sheet. Make statements that support your goals.**

*Note the larger airlines are aggressively pursuing bi-lingual applicants.

Personal Asset Workshop

Verification Statements

Previous Employment ____

____

____

____

Certification/Licenses/Special Training ____

____

____

____

Clubs/Memberships/Organizations ____

____

____

____

Charity/Volunteer Work ____

____

____

____

Hobbies/Sports ____

____

____

____

Personal Skills/Qualities ____

____

____

____

Personal Asset Workshop

Step 3

Place all asterisk items from your "Initial Worksheet" to "Personal Asset Sheet" on the following page. After you are finished if you do not have several items in each category, you may want to spend more time on the workshop. For those of you who are younger or new to the workforce, there are several things in step 4 which you may do to increase your assets.

Personal Asset Sheet

Previous Employment ______________________________

Certification/ Licenses / Special Training ______________________________

Clubs / Memberships / Organizations ______________________________

Charity / Volunteer Work ______________________________

Hobbies / Sports ______________________________

Personal Skills / Qualities ______________________________

Personal Asset Workshop

Step 4. Quick Ways to Increase Your Qualifications

(1) **Take a CPR course** at your local Red Cross or fire department. The courses are usually free of charge and last about eight hours. This is an excellent course that is recommended for everyone. The benefits are tremendous for such a small investment of time. Certification in CPR suggests many things in your favor such as: awareness of life and death situations, quick decision-making, your sense of social responsibility and desire for personal growth. The first flight attendants were required to be nurses, remember?

(2) **Do some volunteer work.** This shows your desire to give of yourself.

(3) **Take a position on an organization** or committee such as a church or condominium board, a fraternal organization, or neighborhood watch group. As a member of a board or a committee, it shows your ability to work within an organizational structure.

(4) **Increase your public contact.** Every airline would like to hire people who have experience working with the public. If your present job doesn't involve heavy customer contact, there are several things that you can do. Transfer to an area of the company that does; change to a job that does; take a part-time job that does. Jobs like waiters/waitresses; salespersons; bank tellers; host/hostesses; ushers; telemarketers or collection officers are just a few of the positions that you can use to increase your public relations experience.

(5) **Volunteer to work on a political campaign.** This is an activity you can easily get involved with. In addition to increasing your public exposure it will familiarize you with foreign and domestic issues. It will also make a positive statement about your character and your ability to support what you believe.

Personal Asset Workshop

These are just a few ways to quickly increase your qualifications. Use your imagination ! There are numerous activities that you can engage in which demonstrate that you possess the most desired traits and public relations skills needed to become a flight attendant. Add these activities to your "Personal Asset Sheet".

Your "Personal Asset Sheet" should be ready to use at this point. You have created an excellent reference to use in all stages of the hiring process. You will want to review your "Personal Asset Sheet" before writing an application request letter, writing a resume, or completing an application. A quick review of your "Personal Asset Sheet" and your verification sentences prior to your interview will give you additional confidence and authority when answering questions concerning your background and qualifications.

Chapter 6
How To Apply

When Should I Start?

Once you have decided to become a professional flight attendant and have gone through the "Personal Asset Workshop" it is now time to apply. Why now? Well, you need to apply now to get the best seniority that you possibly can. Some airlines during peak periods hire as many as 300 flight attendants per month. By procrastinating for just one month, you will allow these same 300 people to be ahead of you for the rest of your career. They will be flying better lines, getting better vacations and making more money!

Getting An Application

There are several ways to obtain an airline application for employment. You can obtain an application by sending a resume and cover letter, an application request letter, asking an employee directly, or by going to the airline ticket counter at your local airport and requesting an application from an agent on duty. In the following section we will discuss the merits of each method. Prior to employing any of these options, check the Airline Information section of this book under "Apply". Many airlines have a telephone number that you can call which provides up-to-date information concerning current hiring practices and the most appropriate methods of obtaining an application.

The Resume

Sending a resume and a cover letter is the most common approach taken to obtain an application. The advantage of a well-prepared resume is that some airlines will call an applicant for an interview after reviewing the information on their resume alone. This can save considerable time over other methods which necessitate waiting to receive an application, returning the application, airline processing of your application and getting a response.

Your resume should be clean, precise and well-balanced. A one-page resume is preferred. If you have access to a word processor or a personal computer, you may want to prepare your own resume. There are several examples of good airline resumes in the reference section. The alternative is to employ a resume preparation service.

The Application Request Letter

One of the fastest ways to obtain an application is the application request letter. This is a very direct letter which provides a little information about yourself and then makes a request for an application. The letter is very effective and it saves valuable time which might otherwise be spent on resume preparation. Although sending a resume is the most traditional approach, all the major airlines have responded with an application when they received an application request letter such as the one in the example. If you do not receive an application within a month try sending a resume, sometimes policies change.

Airline Employment Offices And Ticket Counters

The fastest way to get an application, is to go to your nearest major airport or airlines employment office. The availability of applications at ticket counters varies from city to city and airline to airline.

PREPARING YOUR APPLICATION

Your most important document in the hiring process is the application. Your potential employer must decide if you are special enough for them to engage you in the interview process or send you a rejection letter. You must make your application count. It must be easy for your employer to process. Most applications have five areas. (1) Personal Information (2) Work History (3) Education (4) Personal Qualifications (5) References.

(1) **Personal Data**-This section is self-explanatory. This is the section where you list your name, address and telephone numbers. For telephone numbers, list only those numbers where you can be reached. If you are not accessible during the day at any of your numbers be certain that you have a reliable party to take your messages or that you have an answering machine.

(2) **Work History**-The person who reviews your application will want to see that you have accounted for all of your time during the last 10 years or whatever time frame they

deem applicable. When listing previous employers, make sure that your telephone numbers are accurate and that they include area codes. Contact or visit your previous employer and tell them that you would like to use them as a reference. Ask him or her what they will say when contacted by your prospective employer. People will give you a significantly better reference if you discuss it with them before they are caught off guard by a personnel representative. Quite often the person that you use as a reference will ask you what you would like for them to say about you. How is that for an ideal situation? You will want them to stress your attributes which are essential skills for flight attendants, make sure they stress your punctuality. Have fun! This is your chance to get a perfect reference. Positive references are very important in the interview process.

(3) **Education**-Begin with high school and detail all secondary education. If there is a section for grade point average and you are between whole grades it is generally acceptable to round off to the next highest grade. Use your own discretion in this area.

(4) **Personal Qualifications**-This section is to determine what personal skills you have and to discover why you feel qualified for the position.

(5) **Personal References**-List the names of responsible friends and associates that you have known for at least three years. Include those in different fields such as your religious leader, school teachers ,coaches, close workmates and old family friends.

CREATING A MASTER APPLICATION

Since you will be completing several applications the most efficient way to do this is to compile all of your information in one place. You can do this by completing the Master Application which is located in the back section of this book. The Master Application has all of the categories and spaces that you will find on any company application. Once completed your master application will be an excellent reference. When your airline applications arrive simply transfer the information from your master to the airline application and mail it off. This will eliminate the need to constantly search and assemble information when your applications arrive.

Tips For Completing Your Application

Every application has instructions. Read and follow these instructions carefully. Prior to working on your application, make a duplicate. Complete the duplicated application as you would the original. Either type it or use ink. Completing the copy will first allow you to work out problems that may occur in writing your answers to questions in the limited spaces that you are allowed. Be sure to sign your application and return it with any applicable fees. You might want to include a self-addressed stamped postcard in your application package so that airlines can return this to you confirming receipt of your application.

Waiting For The Calls

You will probably receive a letter or telephone response from your applications in two to six weeks. Once your applications are in, you could be called at anytime, so be prepared. Keep your complexion clear, eat nutritious foods, drink plenty of water and watch your weight! Check your height/weight charts to be sure that you are within limits for the airlines to which you have applied. Many airlines conduct a preliminary weight check prior to the interview. If you are overweight, you will be sent home immediately! You will not be allowed to interview.

Approximately one year ago I helped my niece prepare for an interview. I warned her about keeping her weight in check. Upon arriving at her interview, the first thing applicants were asked to do was to weigh in. She was found to be two pounds overweight. After preparing extensively for the job of her dreams, she was sent home in less than ten minutes ! Get the picture? Don't arrive overweight !

No Response

You should allow from two weeks to four months to hear from an airline. If you do not receive a response in this period of time, you may want to send additional correspondence in the form of a letter indicating your continued interest in the company with an update of your recent qualifications. See sample letters in the Reference Section.

Chapter 7
The Interview

Chapter 7- The Interview

The interview is the most important step that you will take toward reaching your career goal. It should be the focal point of your entire job search. To properly prepare for any interview, you must understand the process and procedures that will be employed so that you will know exactly how to prepare. This chapter will explain the different types of interviewing procedures, questions, and testing practices. This chapter requires active involvement and it includes role-playing, recording responses, information-gathering and

other proven techniques which will give you the knowledge, skill and confidence required to make a well-polished and successful presentation .

Interviews

An interview is a time for both parties to exchange information. It is a time for you to learn more about the company and them to learn more about you. An interview is a process created by a company to evaluate you personally. The interviewers will judge you based on their own feelings, personality test, questions and discussions. The interview process is very subjective and it is often one person making a judgement about another person. Even though precautions are taken to keep the process objective, interviewers like everyone else have good days, bad days, personal likes and dislikes which effect their decision-making process. For this reason it is most important that you develop a good relationship immediately. An interviewer will hire an applicant that they really like over someone who is slightly more qualified but less personable.

Throughout the entire process, you may be discreetly observed by personnel representatives to see how well you interact with the other applicants. It may not always be obvious to you who these representatives are, so act as if you are on an interview from the time you leave your home until the time that you return. Never let your guard down for one minute, not during a meal, a break or even in the rest room!

The elements of each interview largely depend upon the type of interview being conducted. There are three basic types of interviews: the group interview, the individual interview and the board interview. These interviews are often refereed to as first phase, second phase, and third phase depending on the order in which they are given.

The Group Interview

The group interview is normally the first phase of the interview process. The group interview is an efficient way for airlines to quickly preview a large number of applicants at one time. By assembling applicants in a group setting, a company can evaluate their appearance, poise, ability to speak before a crowd, and their interpersonal skills. Group interviews are assembled either by invitation to corporate headquarters or an advertisement for a road show at a local hotel or assembly hall.

The interview begins with each applicant completing a brief information sheet. This can range from just name, address and phone number, to a complete application. This may be followed by a test. The test is usually a brief reading comprehension test to determine if an applicant can understand the company's training material. Once this is complete, the interviewers will introduce themselves and tell you about their airline.

The interviewer will tell you about career opportunities, benefits and future plans of the corporation. After this, each applicant is usually asked to stand and tell the group about themselves and their background. This is your chance to excel. Your introduction should be no longer than 1 minute. You may be given a format to follow or you may simply be asked to tell about yourself and why you want to become a flight attendant. Your introduction should be logical, brief, and informative. Chapter 9 -"Winning the Interview Game", gives an excellent format to follow for personal introductions.

Speak to the interviewers and the entire audience with confidence. Once you have thanked the group and been seated remain quiet and listen intently as your fellow applicants present themselves. It is quite common at this stage for applicants whom are not speaking to be watched to see if they are respectful and attentive to others in the group. Applicants are often disqualified if they are talking are making noise while someone else is talking or introducing themselves.

After a successful group interview, you can expect a personal or board interview either immediately following the group interview or at a later date.

Chapter 7- The Interview

The Individual Interview

The individual interview is the time that the company interviewer will review and discuss your application and work history. Questions may be posed about your past employer relationships, reasons for termination, periods of unemployment and other specifics concerning your background. You might be asked to complete a new application, or you may want to update your present application. The process varies, you may be asked a series of questions or given a written test. Successful completion of this interview may lead to an offer of employment or it may lead to a third or final phase interview.

The Board Interview

The board interview may be either the second or the third phase of the interview process. The board interview or panel interview is considered to be the toughest and most

intimidating. The panel is normally comprised of three to seven company managers from different areas. There will be several people from personnel, a flight attendant supervisor, a manager of inflight services or a senior flight attendant.

The panel members will ask you a series of questions designed to help them determine if you fit the company profile. If you can remain calm and poised in a challenging situation? The questions will help the panel members determine your character, knowledge of the company, your commitment and dedication to becoming a flight attendant.

The Physical Examination

Somewhere during the interview process you will be given a physical examination. During this physical, the company will check your vision, hearing, heart rate, height, weight, blood pressure, or anything else that they deem appropriate. You will also get a blood test which will examine your blood sugar level, cholesterol, and glucose tolerance. Now that drug testing is mandatory for airline crews you should expect a urinalysis.

Chapter 8

Preparing For The Interview

The key to having a winning interview is preparation, knowledge of the process and the ability to present yourself in a way that makes it clear to the airline that you are the ideal person for the job. In this section, I will review the essential areas of preparation.

Gain Knowledge

Before going on an interview, learn as much as possible about the company for which you are interviewing. First check the airline section of this book for the history and general information about the company. Next, go to the library to consult the many publications which can provide you with current company developments. Use the Reader's Guide To Periodical Literature for a listing of recent articles concerning the company. Review articles in publications such as Aviation Week and Space Technology, Dunn and Bradstreets, and Standards and Poors. These are excellent resources for financial information, names of current financial officers, mergers, acquisitions, etc.. ***This may seem a little sneaky but...*** A day or two before your interview, call a stockbroker and tell him/her that you are interested in buying stock in the prospective airline and you would like to know if he/she has any pertinent information. Most major brokerage firms have a wealth of current information on every corporation which each broker can access from his/her desktop computer. Your inquiry will probably result in your receiving the most current and accurate information available concerning that airline.

If you are traveling by air to the interview, read the companies inflight magazine. When you get on the airplane mention to the flight attendants that you are enroute to an interview and you would like to talk with them about the company if time allows. They can be very insightful about the interviewing process and current company information.

Your Weight

Preparing yourself and insuring that you are qualified is an essential step towards obtaining any job. Equally important is to insure that you are not disqualified. Being overweight will definitely disqualify you for a flight attendant job. The following height/weight chart is the most restrictive that we could find. Some airlines allow up to ten pounds over these weights. Most airlines include their own height weight requirements when they send you an application so this chart should be used strictly as a guide.

MAXIMUM WEIGHT FOR HEIGHT

FEMALE HEIGHT	WEIGHT MAXIMUM	MALE HEIGHT	WEIGHT MAXIMUM
5'2"	113	5'2"	127
5'3"	117	5'3"	135
5'4"	121	5'4"	140
5'6"	129	5'6"	150
5'7"	133	5'7"	156
5'8"	137	5'8"	160
5'9"	138	5'9"	166
5'10"	141	5'10	171
5'11"	144	5'11"	177
6'0"	147	6'0"	182
6'1"	151	6"1"	185
6'2"	154	6'2"	190

Health And Appearance

Health and appearance are so closely related that they must be discussed together. Good health is critical to obtaining a flight attendant position for two reasons: 1) to maintain a clear complexion and 2) to pass the companies physical examination.

To be healthy, maintain your ideal weight, and obtain a clear radiant complexion, you must begin practicing good health habits now! Good health can be achieved by learning and exercising an overall healthy consciousness. A healthy consciousness is a change in behavior where one is continually aware that good health is achieved and maintained by combining exercise, rest, and a healthy diet.

Developing a consistent exercise program is required to keep your body firm and your figure proportional. There are probably as many exercise plans as there are diets, however aerobic exercise is most often recommended by healthcare professionals because it increases the heart rate, increases oxygen intake, burns fat, and strengthens muscles. The best results are achieved when an exercise plan is followed at least three times per week.

In 1990 a panel of health experts consisting of five national health organizations and five public agencies condensed their recommendations on healthy eating in a publication called The Healthy American Diet. This book essentially makes seven recommendations for a healthy diet.

Principles for Maintaining a Healthy Diet

1. Eat a nutritionally adequate diet consisting of a variety of foods.
2. Reduce your consumption of fat and cholesterol.
3. Increase consumption of complex carbohydrates and fiber.
4. Reduce the intake of sodium.
5. Consume alcohol in moderation.
6. Achieve and maintain a reasonable body weight.
7. Drink 8-10 glasses of water a day.

Beautiful skin is most affected by diet and skin conditioning. Drinking the recommended eight glasses of water per day is essential to obtaining clear and softer skin. Water increases the bodies ability to eliminate fatty tissues which clog the pores. Blocked pores is the primary culprit in causing skin blemishes.

You must adopt a on-going skin care routine. Deep cleansing, scrubs, moisturizing, and a professional facial should be key elements in your routine.

There is much to know about good health and appearance. Become a lifetime student of health and nutrition not only for your career search but to enjoy a longer and happier life.

ATTIRE

There have been many books written on how to dress for an interview or how to dress appropriately in corporate America. Most of these principles apply to dressing for an airline interview. Your dress should be conservative and professional. Dressing in the colors that the companies' flight attendants wear is not only flattering to the company, but it helps the interviewer to visualize you as a flight attendant which is one of your primary goals.

Women: Always wear a two-piece skirted suit or business dress. Panty hose should be neutral. Your hair should be conservatively-styled. Your shoes should have heels that are low or middle height. Make-up should be just enough to enhance.

Don't Wear...

-sexy, tight or low-cut outfits
-excessive or exotic jewelry
-exotic or masculine hairstyles
-extremely high heels or pumps
-stocking with lace or sexy patterns
-clothes subject to excessive wrinkling
-open-toed shoes
-numerous earrings on each ear

Men: A dark-colored business suit is most appropriate. Your shirt should be white or pastel in color. Your tie should be silk. Your shoes should be dark-colored, simple and polished. Your hair should be neat and not past your collar. A clean-shaven face is most desirable, however, if you have a mustache, it should be trimmed neatly and it should not extend lower than your mouth.

Don't Wear...
-worn or unpolished shoes
-a beard

-dirty or ragged fingernails
-corduroy or denim
-dramatic or trendy hairstyles
-pastel jackets or pants
-earrings

REQUIRED DOCUMENTS AND PAPERWORK

You must be certain that you arrive at the interview with all of the documents that the company requires plus any supportive paperwork of your own. Review your invitation to the interview and make sure that you have all of the documents that are listed. Additionally it would be wise to bring the following documents to any interview:

-a birth certificate
-a copy of your application
-a social security card
-personal/professional references
-transcripts
-a current resume

TRANSPORTATION TO THE INTERVIEW

If you live out of town, most airlines will provide you with transportation to the interview from the nearest city that they serve. If you need to spend the night in that town before the interview, make hotel reservations as soon as possible. There may be hundreds of people in town to interview that day, so space at nearby hotels may be booked. While making your reservations find out if the hotel will provide transportation to and from the interview site. Plan to be at the interview site at least 30 minutes early. **DO NOT BE LATE!!!** If you are even one minute late most companies will not allow you to interview.

Chapter 9

Winning The Interview Game

People often refer to interviewing as a game. When you think of it, its very much like a game, a very important game where your future is at stake. Like any other game to win you must know the rules, practice the fundamentals, and implement a successful strategy. Preparing to play means preparing to win. The rules of the interview were outlined in previous chapters. Your strategy is to present yourself in a fashion that makes it clear that you are the perfect flight attendant candidate. This chapter will provide you with the fundamentals to master. You will learn interviewing tactics, communications techniques, and review sample interview questions. Master the fundamentals, fine-tune your technique, implement these proven strategies and win the job of your dreams !!!

COMMUNICATION

Successful communication is essential to having a successful interview. It is important to understand the elements of communication that are often overlooked. Good communication is not simply the proper selection of words, it is the way that you use your body, your posture, your facial expressions and your voice qualities to convey your message. Effective, sincere communication takes place when all physical and verbal signs are making the same statement. It is important to know that words are the least influential element of communication.

ELEMENTS OF COMMUNICATION

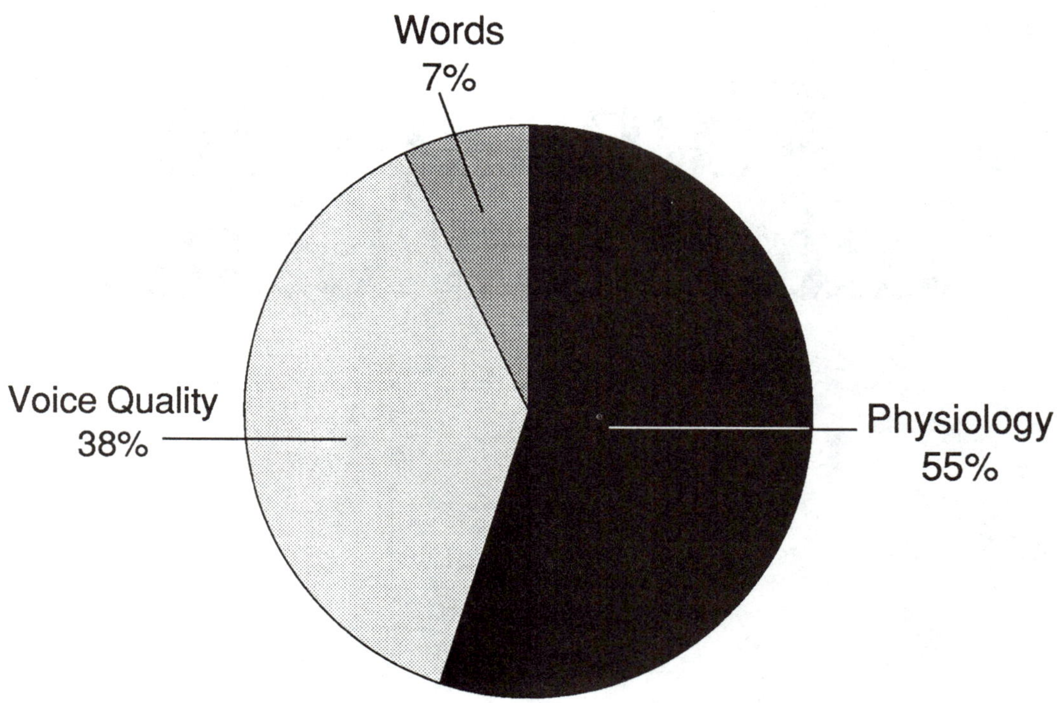

As you can see from the chart physiology is the most influential element of communication, followed by voice quality and then words! People listen to what your body is saying more than the words that you are speaking. Experiment and see for yourself. The next time someone ask you, "How you are doing"? Slouch over, frown, hold your head down, and in your lowest monotone voice say , "I really feel fantastic today." Immediately, that person will become concerned and they will probably ask you what is wrong. That person did not hear you say "I feel fantastic" they heard your body say "I feel lousy". Your appearance and voice tone influenced them much more than your words. The most effective communication is made when your body, voice tones and your words are all saying the same thing at the same time.

At an interview, you want to convey all of the desired flight attendant qualities. What does a friendly, happy, outgoing, independent person look and sound like ? You must always stand tall and erect to exude these qualities. Practice good posture and smile until it hurts! Your voice should be energetic and well-modulated. Use all of the tools of communication throughout your interview process, even when you are not talking.

YOUR PERSONAL INTRODUCTION

There will be many opportunities for you to introduce yourself during the interview process. During the group interview and at several other occasions. Many interviews are started with this statement: "Tell us about yourself." This will be your first opportunity to really sell yourself. Your introduction should range from one to two minutes. Your Personal Asset Worksheet will be very helpful here. The following is a logical format to follow:

Format for Personal Introduction

1. State your full name
2. Where you were raised
3. Where you currently reside
4. Education (Include if it is beyond High School)
5. Your current employer and position
6. Previous employment
7. Special training, skills, or foreign languages
8. Hobbies or special interest
9. Why you will make a good flight attendant

Practice your introduction on a tape recorder. You should sound clear and confident. Your voice should vary, accenting the highlights of your presentation, so it is not monotonous and boring. It should flow smoothly, yet not sound like a prepared monologue. Try it in front of a friend or relative and ask them to critique you. This will help to build your confidence.

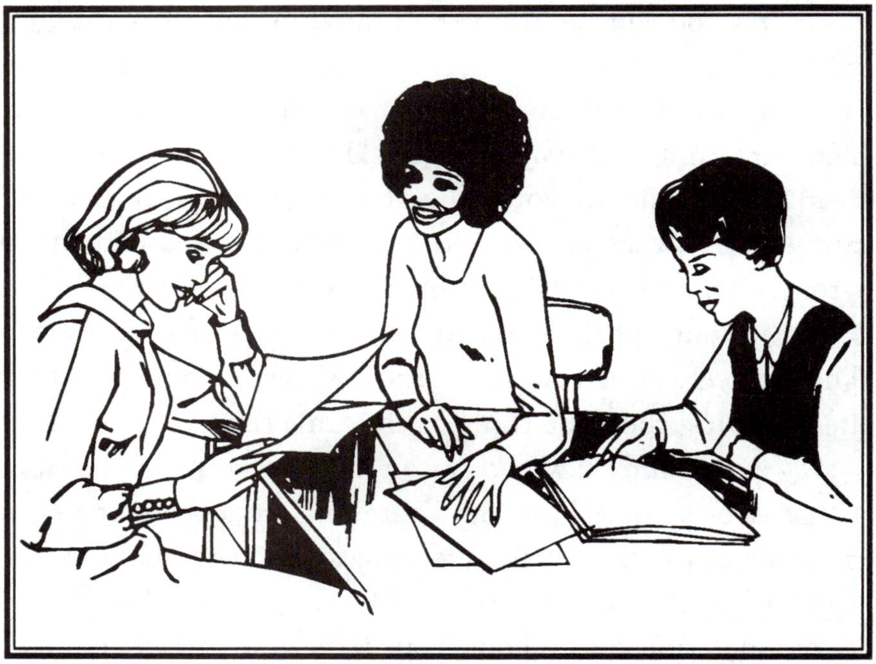

INTERVIEW QUESTIONS AND ANSWERS

The following is a list of questions commonly used during airline interviews. The questions are devised so that the interviewer can learn more about you, what your philosophies are, and how you might react in certain situations. The questions are designed to determine if you really possess the desired qualities that they seek. As you review the list, you will see how each question provides an opportunity to illustrate that you have these special qualities.

The question and answer session is your opportunity to really score points! The best way to practice, is to have a friend assume the role of interviewer and to tape the session so that you can evaluate your responses. This exercise can be a valuable tool in helping you to perfect your style and build confidence.

Answering Questions

-Listen to the question and think about it before attempting to answer it.

- Answer every question in a calm, relaxed manner.

-Be prepared to answer questions which may examine an unpleasant situation such as a termination or an unsatisfactory grade.

-Do not make negative comments about any person or previous employer.

-Answer every question so that it makes a positive statement about you.

-If a question is unclear, ask the interviewer to rephrase it for you.

-Smile whenever an opportunity arises.
-Never question the validity of questions being asked.

Real Interview Questions

Some of the following questions will have answers and explanations to demonstrate how this type of question can be answered to your benefit. Remember, these questions are personal and should help the interviewer to learn more about you.

1. Why do you want to become a flight attendant?
   Example: Because the job seems to fit my personality. I am independent, I love to work with people, and I am particularly intrigued with the variety of lifestyles that flight attendants enjoy.
2. Are you a habitual smiler?
3. What is your definition of customer?
4. Do you feel that you should spoil a passenger?
   Example: Yes, after my primary responsibilities of safety are completed I believe that I should do everything that I can to make my passengers happy.
5. Do you try hard to get people to like you?
6. Do people generally like you?
7. Are you a leader or a follower?
8. Do you feel it is important to pay your bills on time?
9. Do you pay your bills on time?
10. Do you feel that appearance is important?
11. Are you organized?
12. Do your friends and family say that you work too hard?
13. Can you name something fun that you've done lately?
14. What has been the most dramatic experience of your life?
15. Do you like to be in authority?
16. Are you a good listener?
17. Are you a night or day person?

Real Interview Questions (Continued)

18. What is your ideal schedule?
19. Would you spend a lot of money to impress your friends?
20. What is the first thing that you notice when you see a flight attendant?
    Example: Their smile.
21. Why should we hire you?
22. What is your best quality?
23. What are the duties of a flight attendant?
24. What is the most important responsibility of a flight attendant?
    Example: Safety.
25. What will you like most about this job?
26. Can you discuss a public figure you admire?
27. Can you describe the duties and responsibilities of your present job?
28. What is my name? (Do not blow this one!)
29. How do you feel about wearing a uniform?
30. How would you feel about spending Christmas in a hotel room in Iowa?
    Example: Although it would not be as enjoyable as spending the holidays with my family, I am sure that I could have an enjoyable time with my colleagues.
31. Why do you want to work for this airline?
32. Where do you see yourself in the next five years?
33. How will you live on our starting salary?
34. What do you know about this airline?
35. How do you feel becoming a flight attendant will effect your personal relationships?
36. What is your favorite book?
37. What would you do if you spilled a drink on a passenger while serving them?
38. What would you say to a passenger who was afraid to fly?
39. Who was your favorite president?
40. What are some disadvantages of being a flight attendant?

This type of question can be very tricky. Never respond to a negative question with a negative response. Respond like a politician would. **Example:** Most people would consider working a variable schedule to be a disadvantage. It is this variety which attracts me to the job.

In most cases, after you have been subjected to a line of questioning, the interviewer will ask you if you have any questions about the company. Be careful not to ask questions that have already been addressed. Ask questions that imply that you will be hired.

Questions For The Interviewer

-What bases will the next group of new-hires be assigned to?
-Is there anything that I can do now to prepare for training?
-Are there any other opportunities for flight attendants to advance to other positions ?
-How many flight attendants do you plan to hire over the next three years?
-How long will it take for you to notify me of your decision? (Smile when you ask this one)

WRITTEN EXAMINATIONS

During some phase of the interview process, you can expect some type of written test. Airlines use psychological tests, reading comprehension tests, personality tests, on general knowledge and several others. The type of test, and the time it is given, varies from airline to airline. You can prepare for the general knowledge test and reading comprehension test by using any of the college entrance examination testing guides which can be found at your local bookstore. The best way to prepare for any test is to know a few key test-taking principles which will help you to score well.

Test-Taking Principles

1. Listen to all instructions carefully before starting the test.
2. Read any directions that might be printed on the test.
3. If the test is timed, write down the time that you must finished on a piece of scratch paper. If a clock is not in plain view, take your watch and set it on the desk.
4. Preview the test so that you can decide how to best manage your time.
5. On a multiple choice test, if you aren't able to finish, allow a moment to quickly scan through the remaining questions and guess or fill in any answer as time allows. Make sure that points are not deducted for wrong answers.
6. Do not spend too much time on any one question. Write the most probable answer on a sheet of scratch paper and move on. Return to that question when you are finished. If you do not have time to study the question further, you can use the probable choice from your scratch sheet.
7. When guessing at multiple choice questions, begin by eliminating obviously wrong answers first.

8. You will typically have more than enough time to answer questions on personality and psychological tests. Take time to think about them and answer them honestly. They typically ask the same questions in a variety of different ways to determine your sincerity.
9. Do not become obsessed with time.
10. Be confident, you are better prepared than 99% of your competitors.

After The Interview

The first thing that you should do following an interview is to write a follow up or thank-you letter. This is proper business etiquette and it should be considered as part of any interview. An ideal interview thank-you letter should thank the interviewer for his/her time and consideration. It should compliment the interviewer in the way that they conducted the interview, made you feel at ease or whatever you see as appropriate. It should briefly explain how the information and atmosphere at the company has strengthened your desire to work for that airline. A sample "Thank-You" letter is included in the reference section.

At this point you should make certain that you will receive calls or messages at all times. After all of your work, you do not want to miss that most important phone call. An airline may call you the next day to ask you a question that they overlooked during the interview or they may want to offer you the job.

Stay physically fit and form an outline of what steps that you would take if you were ask to move cross-country and start immediately. Be prepared, your new career could literally take-off any day now.

Summary

Several years of work have gone into the creation of this book. I have surveyed hundreds of flight attendants, inflight supervisors, personnel representatives, airline historians, and management personnel to give you what I believe is the most comprehensive and truly helpful guide to becoming a flight attendant ever published.

If you have read the material and completed the exercises you are now armed with information, knowledge, and interviewing techniques which will place you well ahead of most other applicants. Most will approach the interview nervous, uninformed, and ill-prepared. At this point you probably understand the process so well that you, like the company representatives, will quickly spot which applicants have potential and which have not. As you know the people who will be chosen are the ones like yourself, people who display the most desirable flight attendant qualities. Follow the steps in the book, be persistent, and approach your interviews with confidence and enthusiasm. ***Go for it !*** You are about to begin an exiting new lifestyle. Good luck, and I'll see you in the friendly sky's.

Reference

The Airlines

American Airlines

"Something Special in The Air"

Address:	Flight Attendant Recruitment P.O. Box 619410 MD 4125 DFW Airport, Texas 75261-9410		
Number of Employees:	90,000	**Flight Attendants:**	17,000
Stock Exchange:	NYSE AMR		
Fleet Size:	525 +		
Aircraft Operated:	A300, B727, B757, B767, B747, MD-80, DC10, MD11, F100,		
Regions Served:	North-South-Central America, Europe, Caribbean, South Pacific, Far East		
Domiciles:	Chicago, Dallas, Boston, San Juan, New York, Seattle, San Francisco, Los Angeles, Raleigh, Nashville, Miami, San Diego, Washington D.C.		
Union:	APFO Association of Professional Flight Attendants		
B-Scale:	7 yrs.		
Probation:	6 mo.		
Note:	Send self addressed stamped business envelope when requesting an application.		

AMERICAN AIRLINES

In the early twenties a group of investors met to discuss the future of air travel. These men were visionaries, entrepreneurs, who were exited about the future of aviation and convinced that the airplane would change the travel industry forever. To take advantage of the opportunities that this new industry would offer they formed a company called The Aviation Corporation of America or Avco. Avco bought a variety of aviation businesses from flying schools and air mail carriers to barnstorming and crop dusting operations.

AVCOs' many businesses only enjoyed marginal successes until they won the Southern United States Postal Route. To properly serve this transcontinental route AVCO merged a group of over fifty of its' subsidiaries to form **American Airlines in 1930**. Enjoying great success as an airmail carrier, American sought to also compete in the glamorous business of passenger airline service. In planning passenger service American faced a major problem, United Airlines was receiving all of the transport airplanes to roll off of the Boeing assembly line. Instead of just waiting, American took its' problems to McDonnell Douglas Aircraft. At that time, McDonnell Douglas did not make an airplane which could compete with the highly touted Boeing 140, so American Airlines engineers and McDonnell Douglas engineers worked together to develop a competitive airplane. This corroboration resulted in the production of the legendary DC-3. The DC-3 soon became the most successful commercial aircraft of that time. This was the start of a close relationship between American and McDonnell Douglas. American has provided considerable input into the design of several other Douglas aircraft such as the DC-7, DC-10, and the MD-11. The close relationship between McDonnell Douglas and American Airlines continues today.

Here are some key elements in the building of American Airlines:

*1959-began jet service
*1970-Operated first DC-10 in commercial service
*1971-Bought Trans-Caribbean Airlines
*1986-Bought Air California
*1990-Bought Latin American routes from Eastern Air
*1991-Bought TWAs routes to London Heathrow

American is one of the industry leaders. The Airline has enjoyed the top position throughout most of the eighties in areas of size, on-time performance, growth, and efficiency. Winner of numerous service awards American is "*Something Special in the Air*".

Continental Airlines

"One Airline Can Make a Difference"

Address:	ATTN: Flight Attendant Recruitment 2929 Allen Parkway P.O. Box 4607 Houston, Texas 77210-4748
Employment Information:	713-834-5000
Stock Exchange:	Amex CAL
Fleet Size:	375 +
Employees:	35,000 **Flight Attendants:** 8,500
Aircraft :	A300, B727, B737 , B747, MD-80, DC9, DC10,
Regions Served:	North and Central America, Europe, Caribbean South Pacific, Far East
Domiciles :	Cleveland, Denver, Guam, Los Angeles, Houston, Newark, New York, Honolulu, Washington, D.C
Union:	Non-union
Probation:	None
Note:	Send self addressed stamped business envelop when requesting an application.

CONTINENTAL AIRLINES

On April 6, 1926 a gentleman by the name of Walter Varney started an airline.. Varney began flying the mail from Pasco, Washington to Boise, Idaho in a single-seat open cockpit aircraft. Varney became very successful by handling lucrative air-mail contracts. As Varney grew rapidly this success began to threaten it's rivals, mainly Boeing Airlines. Envious of the lucrative route structure that Varney had developed, Boeing bought Varney in 1930.

After the buyout was completed much of Varneys top management were not offered jobs at Boeing, so they formed their own company. This group headed by Robert Six formed a new company which they named Varney Speed Lines. Varney Speed Lines quickly became successful. This airline like the original Varney became an attractive takeover target. In 1937 Varney was taken over by a newly formed **Continental Airlines.**

Continental expanded rapidly throughout the southwest. In 1952 Continental bought rival Pioneer Airlines. And by 1958 Continental went for the major markets flying Chicago to Los Angeles. Throughout the sixties Continental established a reputation of providing superior service.

As all airline stories go the trouble began in the early eighties.
Rising fuel cost and a troubled economy left many airlines weakened and vulnerable to a takeover. At this time Texas International Airlines Chairman Frank Lorenzo was aggressively seeking a merger partner. After an unsuccessful attempt to buy Trans World Airlines, Texas Air hostile took control of Continental Airlines in 1982. Immediately after the takeover management demanded substantial concessions from its employees. This demand resulted in a bitter strike which lasted throughout 1983. The company prevailed. Workers were replaced and the striking workers that did return, returned at half of their former salary.

With lower labor cost and a deregulated Airline industry, Texas Air went on an airline buying binge. Texas Air formed New York Air, bought People Express, Frontier, and Eastern Airlines and a host of commuters such as Britt, Bar Harbor, PBA, Pioneer, and Rocky Mountain.

Although these acquisitions have given Continental a very impressive route structure spanning from Europe to the South Pacific, the cost of these takeovers has burdened the company heavily with debt. To stay competitive Continental has sold a portion of the company to Scandanavian Airlines and is in merger talks with several other carriers.

A merger with another carrier could give Continental the stability and size to compete in todays global market. . Although Continental lacks much of the structure that other employee groups have, Continental employees enjoy a very liberal pass policy, creativity in scheduling such as job sharing, part-time work schedules, and other innovative work rules that are not possible under rigid union contracts.

Delta Airlines
"We Love to Fly and it Shows"

Address:	System Employment Manager P.O. Box 20530 Hartsfield Atlanta International Airport Atlanta, GA 30320-2530
Stock Exchange:	NYSE DAL
Employees:	82,000 **Flight Attendants:** 15,000
Fleet Size:	525+
Aircraft:	A310, B727, B737, B757, B767, DC9, L1011, MD80, MD11
Regions Served:	North America, Eastern and Western Europe, The Far East, Mexico, The Caribbean
Domiciles :	Atlanta, Chicago, Los Angeles, Boston, Dallas, Cincinnati, Salt Lake City
Union:	APFO Association of Professional Flight Attendants
B-Scale:	No B-Scale
Probation:	6 months

DELTA AIRLINES

Delta's beginnings are quite different than that of most other major airlines. Delta's roots can be traced back to Louisiana in 1925 when a company by the name of Huff Daland Dusters was formed to become the worlds first aerial crop-dusting service. In 1928 the company reorganized and changed its' name to Delta Air Service. Delta began passenger service in 1929, flying from Dallas to Birmingham continuing service to Atlanta. In 1941 Delta was awarded a large number of routes from Atlanta. To better serve these routes Delta moved its' base of operations from Louisiana to Atlanta where its' corporate headquarter and largest hub are located today. Here are some key elements to the building of Delta Airlines:

*1925-Huff Daland Dusters Began
*1928-Became Delta Air Service
*1929-began passenger service
*1941-Moved to Atlanta
*1953-Merged with Chicago and Southern Airlines
*1972-Bought Northeast Airlines
*1978-Began Trans-Atlantic service to London
*1986-Bought Western Airlines
*1991-Bought Pan Americans hub in Berlin, West Germany, including extensive routes throughout Europe, the Middle East, and Africa.

Delta has long been known as a conservative airline where employees have enjoyed a family type atmosphere. Delta was able to maintain this close employee relationship because most of Delta's growth had been from within, unlike most airlines which were built through continuous mergers. In recent years Delta has been forced to change its policy of internal growth by acquiring other airlines to expand, since growth has meant survival in the nineties.

Delta is well positioned to prosper in the nineties as a dominate international carrier. Delta boast one of the youngest fleets in the industry and is the recipient of numerous service awards. It is evident that satisfied employees lead to satisfied customers.

"We Love to Fly and it Shows".

Northwest Airlines

Address:	Department H 1470 5101 Northwest Drive St. Paul, Minnesota 55111-3034
Stock Exchange:	Private company. Not traded.
Fleet Size:	375 +
Number of Employees:	53,000 **Flight attendants:** 11,000
Aircraft:	A320, A330*,B727, B747, B757, DC9, DC10, MD-80,
Regions Served:	North America, The Pacific Rim, Europe, South Pacific
Domiciles (Bases):	Boston, Chicago, Detroit, Memphis, Minneapolis, New York, Seattle, Tokyo
Union:	Yes
B-Scale:	5 years
Probation:	6 Months
Note:	Send self addressed stamped business envelope when requesting an application.

NORTHWEST AIRLINES

Northwest Airways was formed October 1, 1926, as an airmail carrier whose first route was from Minneapolis to Chicago. Passenger service began the following year. The following were key events towards the building of Northwest:

*1933-Acquired Northern Air Transport
*1947-Began flying the "Great Circle Route"
*1948-Began the first service to link Hawaii with the Pacific Northwest.
*1979-Began its' first Trans-Atlantic operations
*1985-Bought Republic Airlines for $800 million.
*1989-The company was bought and taken private by an investment group led by financiers Alfred Checchi and Gary Wilson.

Northwest posses the fundamental tools for survival in the nineties. They have a very strong route structure in the profitable Pacific Rim, Trans-Atlantic routes, and dominance in several domestic hubs.

Northwest has been confronted with new challenges since the late eighties. The merger with Republic Airlines and the debt incurred from the recent takeover by Mr. Checchis' group. Once these problems are addressed Northwest will likely settle back into its' former position as an international powerhouse.

Trans World Airlines
"Find Out How Good We Really Are"

Address:	Trans World Travel Academy Flight Attendant Recruitment 502 Earth City Expressway, Suite 204 St. Louis, MO 63045-1315		
Number of Employees:	30,000	**Flight Attendants:**	7,200
Stock Exchange:	Not Available. Private Company.		
Fleet Size:	275 +		
Aircraft :	B727,B747,B767,DC9,MD80,L-1011, A-330*,		
Regions Served:	North America, Europe, Middle East, Caribbean		
Domiciles (Bases):	St.Louis, New York, Boston, Los Angeles, Paris		
Union:	Independent Federation Of Flight Attendants		
B-Scale:	5 yrs		
Probation:	6 mo.		
Note:	Training cost $2,995. Financing available.		

TRANS WORLD AIRLINES

The excitement surrounding Charles Lindebergs' legendary flight across the Atlantic in 1927 was tremendous. While the country became infatuated with adventurous and daredevil pilots, entrepreneurs began to see airplanes as an incredible new business opportunity. In 1928 two gentleman by the names of Jack Fry and C.M. Keys started a company called Transcontinental Air Transport, the beginning of TWA.

One of the teams goals in forming TAT was to capitalize on the growing number of lucrative postal contracts, mainly the transcontinental routes. To win these prized transcontinental routes a company had to prove that they could serve them. To stay competitive Transcontinental merged with Western Air Express to form Transcontinental and Western Airlines or TWA. By the mid thirties TWA was both a successful mail and passenger carrier. They retained Charles Lindberg as a technical consultant. Lindberg not only strengthened the company operationally but his name was also a marketing boom for the company.

In 1942 millionaire Howard Hughs acquired over twenty-five percent of the companies stock and became president of the organization. Howard Hues with his Hollywood mystique and charisma brought tremendous publicity to TWA. It became known as "the airline of the stars" since the countries most prominent celebrities and political figures traveled on TWA.

Using his considerable political influence Howard Hues was able to negotiate valuable international routes. In 1946 TWA became the first airline to offer non-stop service from the United States to Paris. With the addition of many other international routes TWA appropriately changed its name from Transcontinental and Western Airlines to **Trans World Airlines in 1950.** The Airline expanded rapidly throughout the sixties and seventies adding Boeing 727s, 747s, Douglas DC9s and Lockheed L1011s. In fact TWA was the initial customer for the Lockheed L1011.

Investor Carl Ichans offer to purchased TWA was approved in 1985, over a competing offer made by the Texas Air Corporation. This buyout made TWA the only major U.S. Airline to be privately owned at that time. In 1986 TWA purchased its' St. Louis rival Ozark Airlines. Purchasing Ozark Airlines allowed TWA to control over eighty percent of the traffic at its largest hub in St. Louis. Mr. Ichan has recently changed his status as a somewhat passive owner to running the daily operations. The theme of the new corporate identity is to change TWA into a quality low-cost airline for business travelers. The plan seems to be working. TWA's traffic has increased considerably, and the response from business travelers is positive. Carl Ichan has vowed to make TWA a tough competitor and a survivor in the nineties.

United Airlines
"Fly the Friendly Skies"

Address:	Application Processing Center Flight Attendant Employment P.O. Box 6610 Chicago, IL 60666		
Number of Employees:	88,000	**Flight Attendants:**	18,000
Stock Exchange:	NYSE UAL		
Aircraft Operated:	*A320, B727, B737, B747, B757, B767, *B777, DC10		
Regions Served:	North, South, and Central America, Europe, The Fare East, and The South Pacific		
Domiciles (Bases):	Chicago, Denver, Los Angeles, London, Honolulu, San Francisco, Seattle, Miami, Newark, New York, Washington, DC,		
Union:	Association of Flight Attendants		
B-Scale:	5 yrs.		
Probation:	6 mo.		

UNITED AIRLINES

In 1916 an aviation enthusiast by the name of Bill Boeing ordered an airplane from the premier aircraft builder Glen Martin. Martin was so backed up with customers that the wait for his airplanes was well over a year. Bill Boeing became so impatient that he decided to build an airplane himself. A known master craftsman, Boeing did such a good job at building this airplane that people pursued him to build airplanes for them. The more airplanes that he built the more popular that they became. Bill Boeing had found his niche. As business grew Boeing needed a factory. He eventually found the perfect facility, a defunct boating company outside of Seattle. This became the home of the new Boeing Airplane Company.

Already a successful airplane builder Boeing began flying the U.S. Mail. Success in bidding on Government contracts resulted in many lucrative routes. The other major carrier in the region was Varney Airlines. When Varney outbid Boeing on valuable routes to Portland, Spokane, Boise, and Seattle, Boeing became so envious that he bought Varney Airlines. Boeing quickly became a popular passenger airline as well.

In 1930 Boeing Air Transport changed the face of airline travel when the hired a nurse by the name of Ellen Church Marshall to be come the first airline *stewardess.* By 1931 Boeing had merged Boeing Air Transport, Varney Airlines, Pacific Air Transport, and National Air Transport to form United Aircraft and Transportation Company.

The following are key elements to the building of United Airlines:

*Took early delivery of DC-8s
*1960-First to operate B727s
*1961-Acquired Capital Airlines
*1986-Bought Pan American Airlines Pacific Division
*1989-Placed record airplane order with Boeing for $12 Billion
*1991-Bought Pan Ams Hub at London Heathrow Airport
*1992-Bought South American routes from Pan Am

The eighties were turbulent times for United Airlines. Management upheaval, diversity into non-airline interest, employee labor disputes, lack of growth, and lack of corporate direction left United stagnate while more aggressive carriers expanded and took Uniteds market share.

In 1988 United hired Steven Wolf as Chairman and Chief Executive officer. Wolf came on board with a mission to return United to its' former status as a major airline competitor. And that he has done. United has gone from being the slowest growing airline in the middle eighties to the fastest growing airline in the nineties. The financial communities have rallied around Mr. Wolf and his management of the airline. With major expansion in the Pacific, an international hub in London, and the recent acquisition of Pan Americans Latin American operation, United has grown into the worlds largest international airline. Just an all domestic carrier in 1985, United offers tremendous opportunities as the company grows into its' newly acquired international markets.

"Come Fly the Friendly Sky's"

Southwest Airlines

"Just Plane Smart"

Address:	ATTN: Personnel P.O. Box 36611 Dallas, TX 75235-1611		
Number of Employees:	12,000	**Flight Attendants:**	3,900
Stock Exchange:	NYSE LUV		
Fleet Size:	130 +		
Aircraft Operated:	All 737s.		
Regions Served:	The west, midwest, and southwestern regions of the United States.		
Domiciles:	Dallas, Phoenix, Chicago.		
Union:	Association of Flight Attendants.		
B-Scale:	No B-scale.		

Southwest Airlines

In 1967 two gentlemen by the names of Herbert D. Kelleher and Rollin King decided to create an airline very different from anything available at that time. Their concept was to create an airline that would provide safe, reliable, and frequent air transportation at a fair price. After nearly four years of careful planning and administrative work Southwest Airlines began operations in 1971. They started with three Boeing 737's and operated only within the state of Texas. The company has since grown to operate over 125 airplanes to 32 cities in 14 states.

Management at Southwest is dedicated to making the company a fun experience for employees and customers as well. Co-founder Herbert Kelleher is known for his many antics such as, dressing as a woman and visiting the mechanics working the night shift, or painting a 737 like Shamu "the killer whale". Kelleher is much more than a practical joker, his business principles and method of operation have made southwest the most efficient airline in the industry. The company has done what other airlines have only tried to do-achieve a low operating cost, offer reliable service, keep high employee moral while paying wages which are amongst the highest in the industry.

What is most remarkable is that Southwest has been profitable every year since 1972, even during the worst years like 1980 and 1991 when most other carriers were recording massive losses.

Southwest is usually at the top of the list for on-time arrivals and has consistently receive some of the lowest customer complaint ratios in the industry. Recipient of Air Transport Worlds Airline-of The-Year award, Southwest is a great airline and a fun place to work.

USAir

"USAir begins with you"

Address:	Application Distribution Center Employment Services Dept. Washington National Airport, Washington, D.C. 20001
Number of Employees:	48,000 **Flight Attendants:** 9,900
Stock Exchange:	NYSE USG
Aircraft Operated:	B727, B737, B757, B767, DC9, MD80, F28, F100
Regions Served:	North America, Europe, The Caribbean
Domiciles (Bases):	Boston, Baltimore, Pittsburgh, Washington, Philadelphia, Los Angeles, San Diego, San Francisco, Charlotte, Greensboro, Miami, Norfolk,Syracuse
Union:	Association of Flight Attendants
Probation:	6 mo.
Application Fee:	$10.00

USAIR

Usair's beginnings can be traced back to the late thirties, when inventor Lytle S. Adams started an airmail service called All American Airlines. All American was aggressive in the competitive airmail industry. In 1949, All American began passenger service in McDonnell Douglas DC-3's. Flying out of Pittsburgh with most of it's routes through the Allegheny Mountain Region, the company changed its name to Alleghany Airlines, Inc. on January 1,1953. From this point Allegheny would make several well calculated mergers with company's that fit the Allegheny profile. That profile was short-haul routes with limited competition. The first big merger was with Indianapolis based Lake Central Airlines in 1967, followed by Mohawk Airlines in 1972. To reflect its' national presence Allegheny changed its' name once again to USAir In 1979.

USAir was one of the few airlines to remain profitable during the turbulent eighties by monopolizing certain high profit markets. The feeling shared by most airline experts during the late eighties was that an airline must span the globe to remain competitive. USAir did not follow this trend of global expansion. The company continued its current strategy which was to dominate select U.S. markets. To secure its' position on the west coast USAir purchased Pacific Southwest Airlines (PSA) in 1986, and in 1987, USAir bought its' major east coast competitor Piedmont Airlines.

Most airline analyst feel that USAir is destined for yet another merger to gain international routes. However USAir has begun to cautiously expand across the Atlantic. In 1991 USAir bought TWAs' routes to Londons Gatwick Airport. USAir remains a tough competitor in this ever-moving industry. The company has developed a reputation of providing a stable work environment, good pay and harmonious employee relations. *"USAir begins with you".*

Jet National and Charter Airlines

ALASKA AIRLINES

ATTN: Human Resources
P.O. Box 68900
Seattle, WA 98168

Alaska operates a fleet of Boeing 727, 737, and McDonnell Douglas MD-80 aircraft throughout Alaska, the West Coast, parts of Russia, and the Mexican Riviera. Alaska has been noted as one of the nations' most profitable carriers offering high quality service.

ALOHA AIRLINES

ATTN: Human Resources
P.O. Box 30028
Honolulu, HI 96820

Aloha operates a fleet of Boeing 737 aircraft linking the Hawaiin islands.

AMERICAN TRANS AIR

ATTN: Human Resources
P.O. Box 51405
Indianapolis, IN 46251-0405

American Trans Air is a charter airline which operates a fleet of Boeing 727, 757, and Lockheed l-1011 aircraft to many exiting destinations around the world.

AMERICA WEST

ATTN: Human Resources
4000 E. Sky Harbor Blvd.
Phoenix, AZ 85034

America West is a large national carrier which serves over 50 cities throughout the United States and Canada with Boeing 737s, 757s, and Airbus A-320's. Flight attendants have the option to work in other customers services areas.

HAWAIIN AIRLINES

ATTN: Personnel
P.O. Box 30008
Honolulu, HI 96820

Hawaiin operates a fleet of McDonnell Douglas DC-8, DC-9, and Lockheed L-1011 Aircraft throughout the Hawaiin Islands, the South Pacific, and the Mainland United States.

KEY AIR

ATTN: Chief Flight Attendant
P.O. Box 7709
Savanna, GA 31418

Key Air operates a fleet of 727 and DC-10 providing charter service to vacation hotspots.

MIDWEST EXPRESS

ATTN: Human Resources
4915 S. Howell Ave.
Milwaukee, WI 53207

Midwest Express is an airline that was created in 1984 to serve the greater Milwaukee business community. The company provides lavish service to business centers using McDonnell Douglas DC-9 and MD-80 aircraft.

SUN COUNTRY

ATTN: Employment
7701 26th Ave. So.
Minneapolis, MN 55450

Sun Country is a all charter operation which operates flights to Las Vegas,the west coast, and many sunny destinations.

LARGE REGIONAL CARRIERS

Operating

(Jet and Turbo-prop Aircraft)

AIR WISCONSIN

ATTN: Employment
203 challenger Drive
Appleton, WI 54915-9120

Air Wisconsin is a large regional carrier feeding United Airlines in Chicago, Washington D.C., and Denver. Wisconsin displays the United Express logo on its' fleet of F-27's, Dash 8's, British Aerospace ATP's, and its Bae 146 Jets.

AMERICAN EAGLE

American Eagle Recruitment
P.O. Box 610616
DFW Airport, TX 75261-9616

American Eagle is the commuter network owned by American Airlines. Flight Attendant employment for all Eagle carriers is handled through its' central office in Dallas.

ATLANTIC SOUTHEAST AIRLINES

ATTN: Employment
100 Hartsfield Center Pkwy.
Suite 800
Atlanta, GA 30354

A feeder carrier for Delta Airlines part of the Delta Connection, ASA serves smaller markets from its' Dallas, Macon, GA., and Atlanta hubs. ASA operates DHC-7, SD-360, and EMB-120 aircraft.

BUSINESS EXPRESS

ATTN: Human Resources
285 riverside ave.
Wesport, CT 06880

Business Express is part of the Delta Connection. BizEx serves Delta mainly in the northeast using SD-360's,
SF-340's, F-27's, B-1900's. and Bae-146 jets.

COMAIR

ATTN: Recruitment
P.O. Box 75021
Cincinnati, IL 45275

Comair is a large regional carrier which is part of the Delta Connection. Comair serves Delta primarily from its' Cincinnati, and Orlando hubs using EMB-120's, SF-340's, and Canada Air Regional Jets.

HORIZON AIR

ATTN: Personnel
P.O. Box 48309
Seattle, WA 98148

Horizon is a fully owned subsidiary of Alaska Airlines. Horizon has an extensive network throughout the northeast operating F-27's, Dash 8's, and F-28 jets.

WESTAIR

ATTN: Recruitment
5570 Air Terminal Dr.
Fresno, CA 93727

Westair is a United Express commuter who serves United from its' San Francisco and its Denver hubs using SD-360's, EMB-120's, and Bae-146 jets.

Sample Letters

(SAMPLE APPLICATION REQUEST LETTER)

Airlina Crew
757 Jetway Drive
Big Sky, Montana
23677
(504) 354-0000

January 1, 199_

Big Jet Airlines
ATTN: Flight Attendant Recruitment
P.O. Box 747
Airline City, OH 78700

Dear Madame / Sir:

I am seeking a career with Big Jet Airlines as a flight attendant. I am interested in working for Big Jet because I believe that I can make a valuable contribution.

My experience working with the public has been very rewarding. I am a reliable and dedicated worker with excellent communication skills. It has always been important to me to stay healthy, well groomed, and physically fit.

I am eager to exchange additional information with you about myself and my work history. Please send me an application for employment.

Thank you for your time and consideration. I look foreword to hearing from you soon.

Sincerely,

Airlina Crew

Airlina Crew

(SAMPLE INTERVIEW THANK-YOU LETTER)

Janet Jones
100 First Street
Newhire, NY 12221
January 1, 199_

Desired Air
Address
City, State, Zip Code

Dear (Interviewers name):

On (Interview date) I interviewed with you at your corporate headquarters for a Flight Attendant position. It was a most informative and enjoyable process. Visiting your corporate headquarters and interacting with Desired Air employees on my trip to the interview has peaked my interest to build a career with Desired Air.

I want to thank you for your sincere consideration and the open atmosphere which made me feel comfortable throughout the process. If you have any questions or you require additional information please feel free to call me at (212) 222-0000. I look foreword to hearing from you soon.

Sincerely,

Janet Jones

(SAMPLE NO RESPONSE LETTER)

Janet Jones
100 First Street
Newhire, NY 12221
January 1, 199_

Desired Air
Address
City, State, Zip Code

Dear (Interviewers name):

On June 1 of this year I mailed an application to Desired Air. It is now September and I have not heard from you at all. I would like for you to know that I am still very interested in working for Desired Air. I have been working to increase my qualifications since my original application date. I have enclosed a resume which reflects my new accomplishments.

If something has happened and you have not received my application please please mail me another one at the above address.

I want to thank you for your time and consideration. If you have any questions or you require additional information please feel free to call me at (212) 222-0000. I look foreword to hearing from you soon.

Sincerely,

Janet Jones

Janet Jones

(SAMPLE RESUME)

CREWMAN TURNER

2217 Taxi Way
Akron, Ohio 36577
(355) 555-7676

OBJECTIVE:	Career employment as a flight attendant with potential for advancement into training.
EXPERIENCE:	School Teacher: Akron School 57. , Akron, Ohio. Developed curriculum for Junior High Program. (1992-present)
	Karate Instructor: Hiata School of Karate. Akron, OH (1987-present)
	Waiter: Uptown Diner. Winston Park, OH. (1990-1992)
TRAINING:	CPR: Akron Community Hospital. Akron, OH Completed certification April 1991.
EDUCATION:	Ohio State University: , Bachelor of Science Degree, Communications, 1990.
	Willowbrook High School: East Akron, Ohio Graduated Cum Laude, May 28, 1986.
PERSONAL:	Height: 5ft. 10in. Weight: 166 lbs Age: 23 years Marital Status: Single Interest: Reading, fitness, sports, photography, Aviation.
REFERENCES:	Available upon request.
AVAILABLE:	Immediately upon notification.

(SAMPLE RESUME)

AIRLINA CREW

757 JETWAY DRIVE
BIG SKY, MONTANA 23677
(504) 500-5000

OBJECTIVE:	Career employment as a flight attendant.	
WORK EXPERIENCE:	AEROBICS INSTRUCTOR	1992-Present
	Big Sky Work Out Center	Billings, MT
	WAITRESS	1990-1992
	Skyway Restaurant	Bremen, Mt
	SALES CLERK	1989-1990
	Townes Shoppe	Billings, MT
EDUCATION:	MONTANA STATE UNIVERSITY	1987-1990
	Bachelor of Arts Degree	
	MOUNT WAY HIGH SCHOOL	1984-1987
	Bremen, MT	
SPECIAL TRAINING:	PUBLIC SPEAKING	1990
	Speech Dynamics Intl.	
PERSONAL:	Height / Weight:	5ft 7in. / 126
	Birth Date:	December 12, 1968
	Marital Status:	Single
	Characteristics:	Self-motivated, responsible punctual,
REFERENCES:	Personal and professional references available upon request.	
AVAILABLE:	Immediately upon request.	

Commercial Jets

COMMERCIAL JET AIRCRAFT

AIRBUS A300

Description: Twin-engine widebody. Has one engine mounted below each wing.
Range: 4,900
Seats: 265-315. Two aisles.
Flight Attendants: 6-9
Operated by: American, Continental

AIRBUS A310

Description: Looks very similar to the A300 except it is approximately 20 feet shorter.
Range: 6,000
Seats:215-255. Two aisles.
Flight Attendants: 5-7
Operated: Delta.

AIRBUS A320

Description: Twin-engined narrowbody. Has one engine mounted below each wing. Has triangular shaped winglets on each wing tip.
Range: 3,500
Seats: 150-175. Single Aisle.
Flight Attendants: 4-6
Operated By: America West, Northwest
"Nickname": The Electric Airliner

BOEING 727

Description: A three-engined narrowbody with all engines mounted in the back, with the center engine mounted in the tail.
Range: 2,500
Seats: 130-185. Single aisle.
Flight Attendants: 3-5
Operated By: Alaska, American, Continental, Delta, Northwest, TWA, United.
"Nickname": The Three Holer, Seven Two

COMMERCIAL JET AIRCRAFT

Boeing 737

Description: A short and stubby looking twin-engined narrowbody, with each engine mounted below the wing. The engines hang very close to the ground.
Range: 3,500
Seats: 102-149. Single aisle.
Flight Attendants: 3-5
Operated By: Alaska, Aloha, America West, Continental, Delta, Southwest, United, USAir
Other Information: The 737 has overtaken the 727 as the most popular airliner ever produced. There have been over 3000 737s sold. There have been five models of the 737.
"Nickname": Guppy, Thirty Seven.

Boeing 747

Description: A four engined widebody, with two engines under each wing. The Airplane has a large hump in the front of the fuselage which houses the flight deck and an upper level for additional cabin seating. The new 747-400 model has large up-turned winglets on each wingtip.
Range: 8,500
Seats: 325-510. Two aisles. Upperdeck.
Flight Attendants: 8-15
Operated By: American, America West, Continental, Northwest, TWA, United
Other information: The largest commercial airliner built. Has a range of over 8,000 miles.
"Nickname": Whale. Seven Four.

Boeing 757

Description: A sleek narrowbody twin-engined aircraft with very large engines. One mounted under each wing.
Range: 4,600
Seats: 175-225. Single Aisle.
Flight Attendants: 4-7
Operated By: American, America West, Delta, Northwest, United, USAir.

Other: The most efficient airliner ever built.

Boeing 767

Description: A widebody version of the 757.
Range: 7,500
Seats: 210-325. Twin Aisles.
Flight Attendants: 5-9
Operated By: American, Delta, United, USAir, TWA.
Other: The 757 and 767 cockpits are so similar that they are the first airplanes that the FAA allowed pilots to fly both with the same license.

COMMERCIAL JET AIRCRAFT

Fokker 100

Description: Small twin-engined aircraft with the engines mounted on the fuselage in the tail section.
Range: 1600
Seats: 107. Single aisle.
Flight Attendants: 2-4
Operated By: American, USAir
Other: The F-100 is a stretched version of the F-28 which seats 60-80 passengers. USAir is the only major airline to operate the F-28.

Lockheed L1011

Description: Large three-engined aircraft with an engine under each wing, and one in the tail.
Range: 5,800
Seats: 250-380. Twin aisles.
Flight attendants: 5-9
Operated By: Delta, TWA
Other: The L1011 is a very comfortable quite, and efficient airplane which was ahead of its' time. It was first introduced in 1970.

McDonnell Douglas DC9

Description: Twin-engined narrowbody jet with one engine mounted on each side of the fuselage in the tail section.
Range: 2000
Seats: 80-140. Single aisle.
Flight Attendants: 2-5
Operated By: Continental, Delta, Northwest, TWA, USAir.
Other: Although the DC9 is an ageing aircraft which is no longer being produced, it remains a fuel efficient workhorse in many airline fleets.

McDonnell Douglas MD80

Description: A modern and stretched version of the DC9.
Range: 2,700
Seats: 130-165. Single Aisle.
Flight Attendants: 3-6
Operated By: Alaska, American, Continental, Delta, Northwest, TWA
Other : There are five derivatives to the MD80.
MD-81, MD-82, Md-83, MD-87, MD-88

COMMERCIAL JET AIRCRAFT

McDonnell Douglas
DC10

Description: Large three-engined widebody jet with an engine mounted under each wing an one mounted in the tail.
Range: 6,500
Seats: 225-380. Twin aisle.
Flight Attendants: 6-9
Operated By: American, Continental, Northwest, and United.

Other: The "Ten" is an aircraft which has been very popular with passengers, flight crews, and management alike.

McDonnell Douglas MD11

Description: The MD11 is a direct descendant of the DC10. The Airplanes look very much alike except the MD11 has winglets and it is larger than the DC10.
Range: 8,500
Seats: 295-400
Flight Attendants: 7-11
Operated by: American and Delta.

MILITARY TIME

People often refer to the twenty-four hour clock as military time. In airline work one must understand the twenty-four hour clock since it is used in scheduling and utilized by most aviation personnel. As you will see the twenty-four hour clock is simple to understand and it eliminates a great deal of confusion. It is easy to understand the twenty-four hour clock by simply looking at the diagrams below.

As you can see the clocks are the same for the first twelve hours. After 12:00 noon the twenty-four hour clock continues to 13:00 ("thirteen hundred hours") through 24:00.or 00:00

Twelve Hour Clock	Twenty-four Hour Clock
12:00 AM/Midnight	00:00
1:00 AM	01:00
2:00 AM	02:00
3:00 AM	03:00
4:00 AM	04:00
5:00 AM	05:00
6:00 AM	06:00
7:00 AM	07:00
8:00 AM	08:00
9:00 AM	09:00
10:00 AM	10:00
11:00 AM	11:00
12:00 NOON	12:00
1:00 PM	**13:00**
2:00 PM	14:00
3:00 PM	15:00
4:00 PM	16:00
5:00 PM	17:00
6:00 PM	18:00
7:00 PM	19:00
8:00 PM	20:00
9:00 PM	21:00
10:00 PM	22:00
11:00 PM	23:00
12:00 AM/ MIDNIGHT	24:00/ 00:00

Glossary

Airline Terminology/Glossary

Aft: Rear

ATC: Air Traffic Control. The ground-based network of controllers and radar facilities which are responsible for the safe operation of aircraft in flight and on the ground.

ATC Delay: These are delays that occur as the result of ATC's need to separate aircraft by delaying them either on the ground or enroute.

Base: A city that serves as a regional center of operations or a home office for in-flight crews. This is where trips originate and end.

B-Scale: The lower tier of a two-tier pay scale. A lower pay scale where new workers are paid less than their senior counterparts. B-scales typically have a limit of five to seven years.

Bidding: The process of an employee making selections concerning monthly schedules, domiciles or vacations. Choices are awarded to those with the most seniority.

Block Time: The time beginning when the captain first releases the brakes leaving the gate until the time he sets the breaks at the arrival gate. The term blocks originated from the early use of wooden blocks which were wedged under airline tires to prevent movement in the gate area.

Cabin: The interior of an aircraft excluding the cockpit.

Check-In Time: Report time. The time you must report for duty.

Check-Ride: A competency check conducted on a regularly-scheduled flight. This is accomplished through the observation of the crew by company personnel or the FAA.

Cockpit: Flight deck. The forward compartment where the pilots operate the airplane.

Airline Terminology/Glossary

Cockpit Crew: Captain, first officer and flight engineer. Commercial airlines no longer use navigators.

Crew Desk: An area of operations responsible for the day-to-day and long-term scheduling of crews.

Commuting: The process of getting to and from work when you reside in a city other than your home domicile.

Deadhead: A scheduled segment of a trip in which a crew member rides as a passenger, to be repositioned to work a trip or to return home.

Debrief: A brief discussion after a trip where crew members review various aspects of their previous flights.

Diversion: To alter course toward a new destination. Pilots usually divert to an alternate airport when the weather at the planned destination airport is below their landing minimum.

Domicile: See base.

Duty Time: The time that begins when a crew member checks in at the beginning of each day until the debriefing at the end of that day.

ETA: Estimated time of arrival.

FAA: Federal Aviation Administration. The organization which governs the aviation community.

FARS: Federal Air Regulations. A comprehensive list of rules created by the FAA.

First Officer: Co-pilot.

Flight Engineer: Second officer. A licensed pilot who operates and monitors aircraft systems.

Airline Terminology/Glossary

Flight Time: The actual time that elapses from take-off to touch down.

Furlough: Layoff.

Galley: A small section in the cabin where food and drinks are stored.

Gate-Hold: During times of heavy traffic to busy airports the FAA initiates "gate-hold procedures" to hold aircraft at their gates until a specific time when they can take off and fly to their destinations without holding enroute.

Holding Pattern: A racetrack pattern that the controllers request the pilots to fly when the need to delay traffic enroute.

Hub: A city where an airline has scheduled a large number of arrivals and departures, which are coordinated to provide quick and easy connections.

Jumpseat: Special crew member seats.

Layover: The time between your arrival at a destination and your next flight out. This term is used when discussing overnight layovers.

Line: A monthly schedule which outlines your trips and days off.

Maxing Out: If a flight attendant exceeds the maximum monthly hours prior to months' end, he/she gets the rest of the month off.

OPS: Operations.

Pass Ride: Pleasure travel on a reduced rate ticket.

Relief Line: A monthly schedule which is built by schedulers from trips that are open or were dropped for vacation.

Reserve: A status of duty when a crew member is required to be on-call. Reserves need to be available by telephone and ready to be at the airport in a reasonable amount of time. Usually about three hours.

Airline Terminology/Glossary

Second Officer: Flight engineer.

Seniority: A system of employee preference based on date of hire.

Standby: To travel standby. When traveling on a company pass, you are allowed to ride if there is space available.

Taxiway: The paved course around the airport that airplanes to travel to and from the runways, terminals, and hangers.

Turn: Turnaround. Flying to a destination and returning to your point of origin in the same day.

Index

MASTER APPLICATION

The Master Application should be used only as a reference for airline correspondence. Personel information was purposly excluded. **Note:** Making copies of the Master Application is Permissible.

EMPLOYMENT HISTORY

PRESENT EMPLOYER

FULL NAME OF COMPANY | TELEPHONE (AREA CODE) | SALARY: BEGIN | END

FROM: MO./YR. | TO: MO./YR. | ADDRESS | CITY | STATE | ZIP

NAME AND TITLE OF SUPERVISOR | REASON FOR LEAVING

TITLE OF YOUR POSITION

YOUR DUTIES

PART - TIME ________

FULL - TIME ________

HOURS/WEEK ________

PREVIOUS EMPLOYER

FULL NAME OF COMPANY | TELEPHONE (AREA CODE) | SALARY: BEGIN | END

FROM: MO./YR. | TO: MO./YR. | ADDRESS | CITY | STATE | ZIP

NAME AND TITLE OF SUPERVISOR | REASON FOR LEAVING

TITLE OF YOUR POSITION

YOUR DUTIES

PART - TIME ________

FULL - TIME ________

HOURS/WEEK ________

PREVIOUS EMPLOYER

FULL NAME OF COMPANY | TELEPHONE (AREA CODE) | SALARY: BEGIN | END

FROM: MO./YR. | TO: MO./YR. | ADDRESS | CITY | STATE | ZIP

NAME AND TITLE OF SUPERVISOR | REASON FOR LEAVING

TITLE OF YOUR POSITION

YOUR DUTIES

PART - TIME ________

FULL - TIME ________

HOURS/WEEK ________

PREVIOUS EMPLOYER

FULL NAME OF COMPANY | TELEPHONE (AREA CODE) | SALARY: BEGIN | END

FROM: MO./YR. | TO: MO./YR. | ADDRESS | CITY | STATE | ZIP

NAME AND TITLE OF SUPERVISOR | REASON FOR LEAVING

TITLE OF YOUR POSITION

YOUR DUTIES

PART - TIME ________

FULL - TIME ________

HOURS/WEEK ________

PREVIOUS EMPLOYER

FULL NAME OF COMPANY | TELEPHONE (AREA CODE) | SALARY: BEGIN | END

FROM: MO./YR. | TO: MO./YR. | ADDRESS | CITY | STATE | ZIP

NAME AND TITLE OF SUPERVISOR | REASON FOR LEAVING

TITLE OF YOUR POSITION

YOUR DUTIES

PART - TIME ________

FULL - TIME ________

HOURS/WEEK ________

EDUCATION

ATTENDED FROM MO/YR	TO MO/YR	NAME AND ADDRESS OF SCHOOL	MAJOR COURSES STUDIED	DID YOU GRADUATE?	DEGREE RECEIVED	GPA
		LAST HIGH SCHOOL ATTENDED				
		COLLEGE OR UNIVERSITY				
		COLLEGE OR UNIVERSITY				
		OTHER SCHOOL (TECH. VOCATIONAL GRADUATE) AND ADDRESS				

LIST ANY SCHOLARSHIPS, ACADEMIC HONORS OR SPECIAL ACHIEVEMENTS:	EXTRACURRICULAR ACTIVITIES

CHARACTER REFERENCES

NAME	OCCUPATION	ADDRESS/PHONE NO.

SKILLS, AWARDS, QUALIFICATIONS

Notes:

Notes:

Order Form

Order your own copy of COME FLY WITH ME!, or order one for a friend.*

Telephone Orders: Call Toll Free 24 hours: **1(800) JETWAY9.** Have your Visa, Mastercard, or American Express ready.

Or send $15.95 plus $3.00 shipping and handling to:

Maxamillian Publishing
P.O. Box 10034
Chicago, IL 60610 USA

SPECIAL OFFER!!

This coupon is worth $2.00 off on all postal orders. Please send me a copy of COME FLY WITH ME! I am sending a check along with this coupon for $13.95 plus $3.00 for shipping and handling to:

Maxamillian Publishing
P.O. Box 10034
Chicago, IL 60610

Name ____
Address ____
City______________________ State_________ Zip__________

ALL POSTAL ORDERS, PLEASE ALLOW 2-4 WEEKS FOR DELIVERY.

*Community and civic organizations interested in volume discounts should write Maxamillian Publishing "Request Department" on your organization's letterhead.